DINOSAURS RULED!

ALLOSAURUS

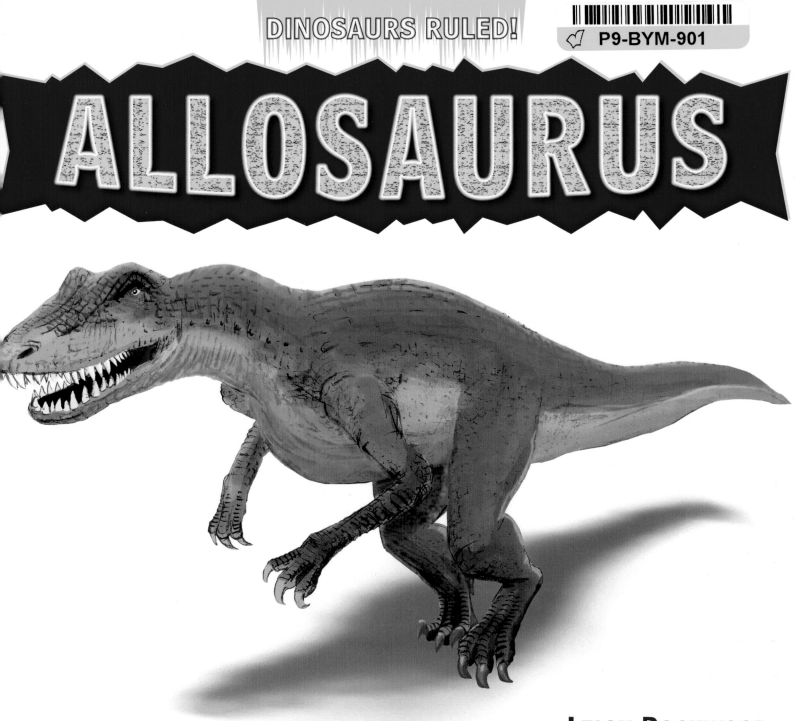

LEIGH ROCKWOOD

PowerKiDS
press™
New York

Published in 2012 by The Rosen Publishing Group, Inc.
29 East 21st Street, New York, NY 10010

First Edition

Editor: Joanne Randolph
Book Design: Kate Laczynski

Photo Credits: Cover, title page by Brian Garvey; cover background (palm tree leaves) © www.iStockphoto.com/dra_schwartz; cover background (palm tree trunk) iStockphoto/Thinkstock; cover background (ginkgo leaves) Hemera/Thinkstock; cover background (fern leaves) Brand X Pictures/Thinkstock; cover background (moss texture) © www.iStockphoto.com/Robert Linton; pp. 4–5, 10, 11, 12–13, 15, 17, 18–19, 20–21 © 2011 Orpheus Books Ltd.; pp. 7, 22 Shutterstock.com; p. 8 Ken Lucas/Getty Images; p. 9 Travel Ink/Getty Images; p. 14 Andy Crawford/Getty Images; p. 16 iStockphoto/Thinkstock.

Library of Congress Cataloging-in-Publication Data

Rockwood, Leigh.
  Allosaurus / by Leigh Rockwood. — 1st ed.
      p. cm. — (Dinosaurs ruled!)
  Includes index.
  ISBN 978-1-4488-4972-7 (library binding) — ISBN 978-1-4488-5094-5 (pbk.) —
  ISBN 978-1-4488-5095-2 (6-pack)
  1. Allosaurus—Juvenile literature. I. Title. II. Series.
  QE862.S3R55525 2012
  567.912—dc22

2011001734

Manufactured in the United States of America

CPSIA Compliance Information: Batch #WS11PK: For Further Information contact Rosen Publishing, New York, New York at 1-800-237-9932

CONTENTS

Meet the Allosaurus

The allosaurus was a large, fearsome dinosaur. This dinosaur might remind you a little bit of the T. rex, which lived millions of years after the allosaurus died out. Both the allosaurus and T. rex were theropods. Theropods were meat-eating dinosaurs that walked on their back legs and had short, armlike front limbs. The word "allosaurus" means "different lizard."

Paleontologists look at allosaurus **fossils** to learn about that dinosaur. Fossil clues let them come up with theories, or ideas, about an animal that has been **extinct** for millions of years.

The allosaurus was one of the largest predators of its time. It had strong back legs and a huge, powerful mouth full of lots of sharp teeth!

THE LATE JURASSIC PERIOD

Did you know that Earth is billions of years old? Scientists use a system called geologic time to organize this long history. The allosaurus lived between 160 and 145 million years ago, which was during the Late Jurassic period.

This graph shows the different periods of geologic time and some of the animals that lived during each time period.

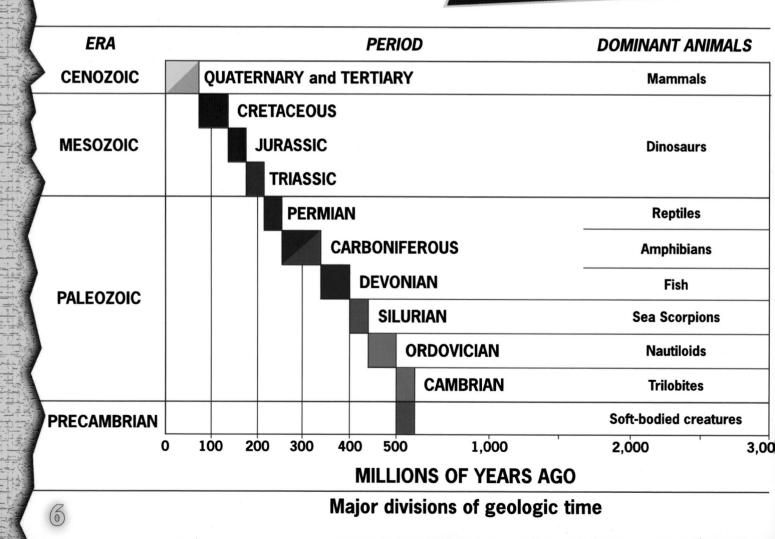

ERA	PERIOD	DOMINANT ANIMALS
CENOZOIC	QUATERNARY and TERTIARY	Mammals
MESOZOIC	CRETACEOUS	Dinosaurs
	JURASSIC	
	TRIASSIC	
PALEOZOIC	PERMIAN	Reptiles
	CARBONIFEROUS	Amphibians
	DEVONIAN	Fish
	SILURIAN	Sea Scorpions
	ORDOVICIAN	Nautiloids
	CAMBRIAN	Trilobites
PRECAMBRIAN		Soft-bodied creatures

0   100   200   300   400   500   1,000   2,000   3,000

MILLIONS OF YEARS AGO

Major divisions of geologic time

The picture on the left shows how the continents looked when they were all one landmass. By the end of the Late Jurassic period, Pangaea had begun to break up, as shown in the image on the right.

The world looked very different during the Late Jurassic period. All of Earth's **continents** were one landmass, called Pangaea. This large landmass began to break apart by the end of the Late Jurassic period. The **climate** was warm during this time period. Plentiful plant life fed the plant-eating dinosaurs, such as the stegosaurus, that the allosaurus hunted.

WHERE DID THE ALLOSAURUS LIVE?

Fossils form in **sedimentary rocks**. Sedimentary rocks form when layers of mud, sand, or stone are pressed together over millions of years. Fossils form when dead plants or animals get trapped in these layers of sediment. The western United States has many sedimentary rock

This model shows an allosaurus among the trees and ferns of its Jurassic habitat. A habitat is all the plants and animals that live in a place.

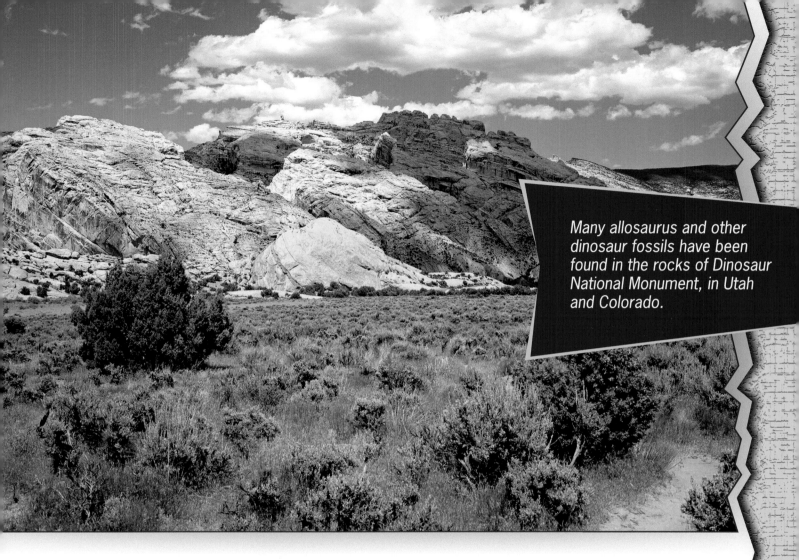

Many allosaurus and other dinosaur fossils have been found in the rocks of Dinosaur National Monument, in Utah and Colorado.

formations. Fossils from many dinosaurs have been found there.

Allosaurus fossils have been found in Wyoming, Utah, South Dakota, Montana, New Mexico, and Colorado. Today much of this area is dry and desertlike. During the Late Jurassic period, these lands were warm, **humid**, and full of different kinds of plants.

The Allosaurus's Body

A full-grown allosaurus was about 35 feet (11 m) long from head to tail. The dinosaur was heavily built, too. The allosaurus walked on its strong back legs. Its front limbs were much shorter. They were not used for walking. Each

The allosaurus walked on its large back legs. Its tail was held straight out behind it for balance.

You can see that the allosaurus walked on the toes of its hind legs here.

front limb had a three-fingered hand with sharp, 6-inch (15 cm) claws at the end. It likely used its hands to grab things or kill **prey**.

Half of the allosaurus's body length was made up of its tail. This long, strong tail helped the dinosaur keep its balance as it chased prey.

FALLING DOWN

Paleontologists think that dinosaurs like the allosaurus could not run without being in danger of hurting themselves. If you trip while you are running, your hands often help break your fall. Because the allosaurus had such short arms, it could not do this. Instead, it would take a nasty fall.

X-rays of fossilized allosaurus skeletons have shown places where the dinosaurs' ribs had broken and

The allosaurus was a theropod, and all theropods had short front limbs. They were too short to be used for much. These limbs may have held on to food that was moving around a lot, though.

then healed. These broken bones are believed to have come from falling over while running. Since the bones healed, it shows that these running falls would have hurt allosauruses but not killed them.

BUMPY HEAD

The most noticeable things on the allosaurus's skull were the brow horns and bony knobs. These bumps started over each **eye socket** and formed a ridge that ended at the tip of the dinosaur's snout.

Paleontologists are not sure what purpose these bony growths may have served. They have a few

Do you see the bony bump on top of this fossilized allosaurus skull? There are a few smaller ridges right in front of the large bump, too.

Compare the shape of this allosaurus's head to the skull on p. 14. Paleontologists use the shape of the skull and other bones to tell them how a dinosaur might have looked.

theories, though. The bony growths may have helped keep the allosaurus's eyes safe when it fought other dinosaurs. The bony growths also could have helped identify male and female allosauruses. This would be useful when an allosaurus was looking for a **mate**.

BIG TEETH

The allosaurus had a large set of powerful jaws with around 30 sharp teeth. These teeth were between 2 and 4 inches (5–10 cm) long.

The allosaurus's teeth were pointed and had sawlike edges. On the upper jaw, the teeth curved toward the inside of its mouth. The teeth on the lower jaw were

Can you imagine seeing a mouth full of teeth like these coming toward you? A bite from an allosaurus was something most dinosaurs worked hard to avoid!

Here you can see how the allosaurus's top teeth curved in. It could open its mouth wide to bite into its prey with its top teeth. It would then close the bottom jaw and start eating.

a bit straighter. The different directions of the teeth made the dinosaur well suited to eating meat. First, the allosaurus could get a deep bite with its upper teeth. Then it could use the lower teeth to tear the flesh from its prey.

A Meat-Eating Dinosaur

The allosaurus was a **carnivore**. A carnivore is an animal that eats only meat. The allosaurus was the biggest **predator** in its Late Jurassic period home.

The allosaurus most likely preyed upon plant-eating dinosaurs like stegosauruses. It also likely preyed on larger dinosaurs like

Allosauruses would hunt and kill prey, but they would also eat prey that was already dead. Huge dinosaurs needed a lot of food. They could not be picky!

apatosauruses if they were sick or injured. This would give the allosaurus a better chance of killing these much larger dinosaurs. It is also likely that the allosaurus was a **scavenger**. Like most carnivorous dinosaurs, the allosaurus was not a picky eater. Whatever it could catch or kill, would be dinner!

DINO BITE

Like many meat-eating dinosaurs, the allosaurus's brain was fairly large compared to the rest of its body. This leads paleontologists to believe that the allosaurus was one of the smarter dinosaurs.

Teaming Up

The allosaurus was the most plentiful predator of its time. It is thought that the allosaurus did most of its hunting alone. The dinosaur could have hidden among thick-growing plants and waited to attack its plant-eating prey.

Some paleontologists believe that the allosaurus sometimes hunted in groups. By hunting in a pack, allosauruses could prey upon much larger dinosaurs like the diplodocus or the camarasaurus. Scientists came up with this theory after finding more than one set of allosaurus footprints in the same place. Other scientists do not think these footprints meant the animals hunted together. Instead those scicentists think they scavenged and ate the same dead dinosaur at different times.

Some scientists think allosauruses hunted in a pack when hunting large dinosaurs, as shown here. They had a better chance of killing a large dinosaur if they worked together.

No Bones About It

A rancher named Marshall Felch found the first nearly complete allosaurus skeleton in Colorado in 1883. More than 60 allosaurus fossils have been found since that time. Most of these have been found in the Morrison Formation. The Morrison Formation is a series of sedimentary rock layers that lie mostly in Colorado and Wyoming. This area is rich in Late Jurassic period fossils.

Dinosaur bones are not the only part of the animal that can become fossilized. Fossilized eggs, such as these, footprints, and even waste are all important finds!

Each time a new fossil is found, paleontologists have a chance to learn new information about a dinosaur's diet and how it lived, even though it has been dead for millions of years.

GLOSSARY

carnivore (KAHR-neh-vor) An animal that eats only other animals.

climate (KLY-mut) The kind of weather a certain place has.

continents (KON-tuh-nents) Earth's large landmasses.

extinct (ik-STINGKT) No longer existing.

eye socket (EYE SO-ket) A hole in the skull where one eye sits.

fossils (FO-sulz) The hardened remains of dead animals or plants.

humid (HYOO-med) Damp or moist.

mate (MAYT) A partner for making babies.

paleontologists (pay-lee-on-TAH-luh-jists) People who study things that lived in the past.

predator (PREH-duh-ter) An animal that kills other animals for food.

prey (PRAY) An animal that is hunted by another animal for food.

scavenger (SKA-ven-jur) An animal that eats dead things.

sedimentary rocks (seh-deh-MEN-teh-ree ROKS) Stones, sand, or mud that has been pressed together to form rock.

X-rays (EKS-rayz) Special pictures that can be taken of the insides of bodies.

INDEX

WEB SITES

Due to the changing nature of Internet links, PowerKids Press has developed an online list of Web sites related to the subject of this book. This site is updated regularly. Please use this link to access the list:
www.powerkidslinks.com/dinr/allo/